A WOMAN'S
LITTLE INSTRUCTION BOOK
VOLUME II

A Woman's
Little Instruction Book
Volume II

Jasmine Birtles

B◼XTREE

First published 2000 by Boxtree
an imprint of Macmillan Publishers Ltd, 25 Eccleston Place, London SW1W 9NF, Basingstoke and Oxford

www.macmillan.co.uk

Associated companies throughout the world

ISBN 0 7522 1807 7

Copyright © 1999 Jasmine Birtles

The right of Jasmine Birtles to be identified as the author of this work has been asserted by her in accordance
with the Copyright, Designs and Patents Act 1988.

All rights reserved. No part of this publication may be reproduced, stored in or introduced into a retrieval system,
or transmitted, in any form, or by any means (electronic, mechanical, photocopying, recording or otherwise) without the prior written permission of the publisher. Any person who does any unauthorized act in relation to this
publication may be liable to criminal prosecution and civil claims for damages.

1 3 5 7 9 8 6 4 2

A CIP catalogue record for this book is available from the British Library.

Designed by Nigel Davies. Printed by Caledonian.

Illustrations by Sue Clarke.

This book is sold subject to the condition that it shall not, by way of trade or otherwise, be lent, re-sold, hired out, or
otherwise circulated without the publisher's prior consent in any form of binding or cover other than that in which
it is published and without a similar condition including this condition being imposed on the subsequent purchaser.

If you were labouring under the impression that it's tough being a woman, worry no more. Being a woman is not a medical condition – whatever the magazines try to tell you. Face it, there are lots of reasons why it's great to be a woman: no prostate problems, no interest in picking up a man at a night bus-stop and a variety of different moods to enjoy throughout the month. These and other exciting aspects of a woman's life are all covered in this fab, fun book of instructions for the woman of today. And remember, love means never having to say you're sorry. So does being a bastard.

Wine, women and song
all improve with age.

Become a mad old crone –
a shopping trolley full of all your
possessions will never let you down.

Don't go fox-hunting.
Have it delivered.

Sleep with him in haste,
repent at the clinic.

Plastic surgery –
having your credit cards
cut up.

Don't go after your
best friend's husband.
He's no prize as you should
know having listened to her complaints
for the last few years.

Women's magazines are such a joy.
Where else can you learn how to be a
strong independent woman
while at the same time being a
14-year-old, moody anorexic?

If you can name
any character from
any daytime TV soap,
it could be time to have
yourself put down.

There is something missing
in your life if you look forward
to dental appointments –
unless your dentist looks
like George Clooney.

Don't get a
permanent tattoo,
have temporary ones –
but remember
they're not iron-on.

Develop any incipient lunacy –
men always say we're mad
anyway so hey, go with it.

When you say 'I love you'
don't expect your cat to respond.

Don't let a little friendship
ruin a good feud.

Count your age
in dog years.

Act like a queen –
never carry money, have no dress sense
and only speak at Christmas.

If he wants to sow some wild oats,
start the threshing machine.

Don't be a fashion slave –
chains and manacles
haven't been in since the dark ages.

A man's eligibility is in inverse proportion
to the number of his tattoos.

If you get divorced make sure
you have custody of the money.

Spend time alone. The company
is the best you'll ever find – possibly
the only company you'll ever find.

Be different –
have your pancreas pierced.

Housekeeping tip: if he leaves you,
keep the house.

Dangerous men
to consider marrying:
rock stars, film stars, ad-men,
marketing men, writers,
artists, your father.

Feng Shui your
husband – put him
in the place where
he can make the
most money.

Reincarnation
can't be true.
If it were we wouldn't
keep marrying the
same mistakes.

Remember,
to get promotion
you have to have
cleavage, sorry,
qualifications.

How to make him hate you:
say 'it's only a game'.

Love is a two-way street but
more and more people jay-walk.

A married woman is just a single woman
with less shelf-space.

Never turn your back on your girlfriends.
You can't trust them that much.

He's not impressive if he's just
been voted 'man of the year' by the
Brewer's Association.

Cellulite: proof that when
you reach the bottom it can get worse.

A husband is for life,
not just for Christmas, so don't go mad
on his presents.

Without talent you can only
sleep your way to the middle.

If you want a partner who'll be loyal,
dependable and loving, get a St Bernard.

Love is a two-way street. You can be
driven crazy coming and going.

Remember, there are plenty of fish in
the sea – it's just that most are flounder.

G-strings: proof that fashion
really is up its own arse.

The most common cause of love
at first sight is a badly lit room.

To find your prince charming
you have to kiss a lot of toads.

Always buy women's magazines – they're
fantastic for lining the cat-tray.

If love is so blind, how come we
spend so much on cosmetics?

Try computer dating – you might meet
someone nice if the computer
doesn't turn up.

Being a woman is not
a medical condition.

You know he's a loser if
he asks if you take credit cards.

There are seven ages of man
but only three ages of women –
child, 21 and 'not telling'.

If he says he can't live without you
he's not sweet, he just can't feed himself.

If you want a boyfriend as an
accessory you'll probably be the first
to go out of fashion.

Reasons it's great to be a woman:
no prostate problems,
not bothering to pick up a man
at a night bus-stop and
a variety of different moods to enjoy
throughout the month.

Never kick a man when he's down.
Step over him – you'll get further.

It's always better to give than to receive –
especially if it's grief.

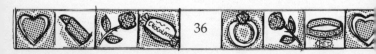

Love is blind so take a labrador.

Therapy is expensive.
Popping bubblewrap is cheap.
You choose.

Be adventurous.
Try a new position
with your man tonight:
him over the kitchen sink
and you in front of the telly.

Diamonds can't be
a girl's best friend.
Who ever heard of
a diamond going off with
someone's husband?

Always ask your friends
for advice about your man.
It passes the time and
gives you someone to blame
when it all goes wrong.

You're reading
too many magazines
if you're worried because
you don't have
any symptoms.

Follow fashion – if only to
laugh at the photos in later years.

The only colour therapy worth
bothering with is the colour of money.

To control a man use dog-training
methods: put him on a short lead
until he's learnt not to stray,
keep him off the good furniture
and pretend he's not yours if he
tries to lick his balls in public.

Women are like cats:
they're fussy about their food,
they like to toy with lesser creatures
and they can get their claws out
when you least expect it.

If you need
self-help books
to tell you what to do
with your life you're
missing the point.

Going out with a man
out of morbid curiosity
is not a good start
for a relationship.

Trust me,
'I just need some space'
doesn't mean he wants
to become an astronaut.

Tell people you are
older than you actually are.
That way they'll be impressed
at how young you look.

Men love to collect
facts and figures –
mostly sporting facts and
well-proportioned figures.

You can't make him
love you but you can make his life
a misery for not doing so.

You are not fat.

Unfaithful men often leave clues –
a hotel credit card receipt,
a sudden need to work late in the office
and the words 'I'm sleeping with
someone else' sprayed in four-foot
letters on your bedroom wall.

Really good opener for
making him listen: 'Have you
ever thought of fatherhood?'

Bad opener for making him listen:
'Let's talk about our feelings.'

The best way a man can
help around the house is by
buying you one.

Encourage your inner child.
It'll give your man someone to talk to.

Don't expect him to
notice every change of hairstyle.
If he notices his own change of
underwear he's doing well.

Even if you look like
Frankenstein's mother you can
still get a man by not interrupting
when he speaks.

You know you're getting on
when your children and your clothes
are the same age.

We all spring from animals but some men
didn't spring far enough.

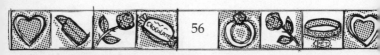

Depression:
nature's way of telling
you to watch more TV.

There are two sides to every argument,
until you take one.

Some men are thinkers,
some men are sexy,
others are a cross
between the two –
they just think they're sexy.

How to tell whether he's
in love with you:
1) Has he made you a
compilation tape?
2) There are no other signs.

Good opening lines:
'I need some help choosing the
right stereo system,'
'Could you do this dress up?' and
'Do you know, I can get drunk on
one glass of wine.'

Never trust a man who has
a penchant for cravats.

A single woman is just a married woman
who has to look after her own car.

Rule of life:
you will always meet
your ex-boyfriend when you're
wearing sweatpants, no make-up
and a freak acne rash.

Plastic surgery –
assaulting your husband
with tupperware.

Men will pay to see women naked.
Women will pay for men to
put their clothes back on.

Never learn how to iron.

Practice random acts of intelligence and
senseless moments of self-control.

A woman's favourite position
is CEO.

If you want to hear
the pitter-patter
of tiny feet, put shoes
on your cat.

You should marry him
if he's never heard of cellulite,
thinks you're too thin and believes that no
woman should do housework.

If you want to look younger
hang around with older men.

Plastic surgery: something that
makes you look ten years' scarier.

Don't stand still too long in Soho.
You'll get your nipples clamped.

Love means never having to say
you're sorry. So does being a bastard.

Never be the first to say
'I love you' –
you'll just hear the hollow echo
in the ten minute silence
that follows.

You know you're
getting on when all your bits
have gone south for the winter …
and the summer …
and the spring …

Childish behaviour:
him hiding the remote control
when you want the
shopping channel.

There are lies,
damned lies, and all that stuff
blokes tell each other
down the pub.

Go for short, bald men –
they try harder.

Sugar daddies are for women who have
everything but can't afford to pay for it.

Anti-ageing creams:
the triumph of hope over experience.

Work in a bank. They have everything
a woman needs – money and holidays.

Figures don't lie but lycra
redistributes the truth.

Be charitable and always remember the
poor – it doesn't cost you anything.

If your man can't see why you're
wearing a strapless dress then don't.

Money can't buy you everything
but credit cards get close.

Don't look for a husband,
just go out with single men.

Show me a woman with a perfect
figure and I'll show you a woman who'd
kill for a bag of chips.

What to say when your mum
asks why you're not married yet:
1) I think it would take the fun
out of dating,
2) I have enough laundry as it is,
3) I wouldn't want you to drop dead
out of sheer happiness.

Kill your speed. Also throw out
your E, crack, PCP's, blow and heroin.

See no evil, hear no evil,
date no evil.

Smoking gives you
wrinkles, as do drinking,
scowling and worrying.
So which ones was
Mother Theresa doing?

Hysteria comes from the
Greek word for 'womb',
like the Old English word
for the medical history of women
which is, of course, 'bollocks'.

If you think that
having bad breath, saggy skin,
poor respiration and no money
is attractive,
take up smoking.

If he kisses with his eyes open
it could be he's checking to see
if his wife's in the room.

Laugh and the world laughs with you.
Fart and you sleep alone.

Never admit to being able
to change a tyre. They have to feel
superior at something.

Every woman should be financially
solvent, not tearfully dissolvent.

The female body has
thousands of muscles which
are there specifically to let us know
that we shouldn't have done that
extra hour of aerobics.

Be kind to assistants on
beauty counters. They must have
had some terrible tragedies in
their lives to turn them into such evil,
confidence-destroying bitches.

You can tell when a beautician
walks into the room because her make-up
arrives five minutes before she does.

If he brings home flowers for no reason,
there's a reason.

Love is like a steamroller.
Even if you see it coming from
a mile off it can still knock you flat.

Play hard to get. Wait an extra ring
before you pick up the phone.

When a man goes on a date
he wonders if he's going to get lucky.
A woman already knows.

Women still remember the first kiss
after men have forgotten the last.

Men's magazines
have very little advice
because men think they
don't need it. They say
'I know what I'm doing.
Just show me someone naked.'

A man loses his sense of direction
after four drinks.
A woman loses hers after four kisses.

Never take men seriously – they're only
there to keep us entertained.

When women
refuse to get married
we call it independence.
When men refuse we call
it lack of commitment.

Only two things are
necessary to keep
your husband happy.
One is to let him think he is
having his own way and the
other is to let him have it.

Anyone who says women are
the bitchiest sex has obviously
never been in a gay bar.

Take up schizophrenia.
That way you'll never be lonely.

Stony silences and
cold looks won't punish him.
Just start wearing a pair of
large, greying pants and a
reinforced bra and he'll get the idea.

Don't imagine that
the battle for equality is over.
Men still have a long way to go
to reach our standard.

Mothers always
feel sorry for non-mothers
because they have no children.
Non-mothers feel sorry for mothers
because they do.

At a party, don't talk about yourself.
That'll be done after you leave.

It's a bad sign if you marry a playboy
and his friends give you matching
towels marked 'His' and 'Next'.

In olden times witches were burnt
at the stake. Now they just run
Human Resources departments.

You know he's a loser if he's not in
Who's Who but did make *What's That*.

You need a personality boost
if you go in for computer dating and they
match you with a tub of lard.

The day your mother approves of your
hairstyle it's the beginning of the end.

Don't believe in free love.
It's just marketing speak for him
getting his own way.

Be careful with step-children. Don't
try and finish what you haven't started.

One good turn gets
most of the duvet.

There's nothing wrong with any
relationship that a discussion with
your girlfriends can't worsen.

Diets don't work
but worry, chronic depression
and panic attacks shed pounds.
So what are you waiting for?
Get neurotic.

Try some dangerous sports:
standing in front of the TV during
the FA Cup Final, giving his oldest,
tattiest jumper to the charity shop and
washing his car with a brillo pad.

If he hasn't phoned
after two days don't worry.
If he hasn't phoned after
three days that's still OK.
If he hasn't phoned after four days
you probably should have had
your moustache waxed.

If he hasn't phoned within a week he's probably been held hostage.

If he hasn't phoned after a month... hang on, you didn't get round to giving him your phone number did you.

Always take suncream on the beach.
It gives you an excuse to chat-up a lifeguard.

Cake –
nature's answer to Prozac.

Better to have loved and lost
than to be lumbered with a loser.

If you like men in uniforms
have yourself arrested.

Rule of life:
the night you
can't be bothered to go out
your hair will be looking too good
to stay in.

Rule of life:
it always takes
two hours longer to make yourself
look natural than it does
to look glam.

If you're on the rebound
your taste in men will be terrible.
That's also true if you've been
drinking or dieting, or if
you are pregnant …

… menstruating, tired,
emotional, pissed-off, bored,
desperate, unhappy, happy,
rich, poor, old, young
or just plain female.

Women are the stronger of the sexes.
Thousands of years being left holding the
baby has really built up our muscles.

Don't be afraid to take risks.
Let him cook dinner once in a while.

When approaching a man,
be confident. If you can be semi-naked too
that'll give you a real head start.

All work and no play makes a normal day
for a working mother.

Being dumped:
nature's way of telling you that you're
just too darned good for that git.

If you really want to worry him why not
buy flowers for him some time?

To get close to a man
copy his breathing patterns –
unless he's the sort who rings
you up to say 'I'm watching you',
'I know where you live…'.

Watch your
alcohol consumption.
Better to drink yourself
under the table than under
the nearest man.

Equal opportunities
means you have
the opportunity to divide your
entire life equally between office work
and housework.

When you meet a man
you have to have faith, hope and charity.
Faith that he'll be good,
hope that he won't cheat
and charity if he does.

Inside some of us is
a thin person struggling
to get out, but she can
usually be placated with
a few pieces of chocolate cake.

Life is an endless struggle
full of frustrations
and challenges, but eventually
you find a hairdresser you like.

One of the life's mysteries
is how a two pound box
of chocolates can make a woman
gain five pounds.

Time may be a great healer,
but it's also a useless beautician.

Brain cells come
and brain cells go,
but fat cells live forever.

The only time a woman wishes she were a year older is when she is expecting a baby.

What's the worst thing
about having a colostomy bag?
Finding shoes to match.

One of the wonders
of science: you just
hang something in your wardrobe
for a while and it
shrinks two sizes.

Statuesque, percipient, gregarious – these are just three of the words that Jasmine Birtles has difficulty spelling. A former model – for Airfix – Jasmine has spent the last 20 years living under an assumed hairstyle. As she will tell anyone who'll listen, she was a child prodigy. Unfortunately, she was also a late developer, so no one knew until it was too late. She's a collector of pocket fluff, nasal hair and those complimentary sachets of coffee whitener you get on airlines, but has been told to stop it by her mother. An amateur acupuncturist, she knows nothing of pressure points and chi energy, she just likes sticking needles into people.